NARROW GAUGE ON THE ILE DE RE AND THE ILE D'OLERON

PETER SMITH

Copyright © 2013 Peter Smith

All rights reserved.

ISBN-10: 1493578863

ISBN-13: 978-1493578863

CHAPTERS

ILE DE RE

1. INTRODUCTION   Page 1

2. THE ISLAND   Page 2

3. THE RAILWAY   Page 6

4. SABLANCEAUX PIER   Page 10

5. ALONG THE LINE   Page 16

6. ST MARTIN DE RE   Page 24

7. LOCO'S & ROLLING STOCK   Page 36

IL D'OLERON

1 INTRODUCTION   Page 47

2 BACKGROUND   Page 50

3 THE RAILWAY   Page 52

4 ALONG THE LINE   Page 55

5 ST TROJAN MINATURE RY.   Page 65

CHAPTER 1

INTRODUCTION

A self-contained narrow gauge railway on an island is always an appealing prospect, and the line on the French island of Ile de Re was a delight. As with most of these narrow gauge railways it became increasingly out of step with life as the twentieth century progressed and couldn't survive - average speeds of 12km an hour didn't help!

Fortunately the railway was well served by photographers producing postcards and this book will I hope serve both a record of what existed and as an inspiration for modellers.

CHAPTER 2

THE ISLAND

The Ile de Re is an island located in the Atlantic ocean off the coast of France close to La Rochelle. Part of the Charentais archipelago, it is the fourth largest island in metropolitan France behind Corsica, the Ile d'Oleron and Belle Island. Formerly an integral part of the province of Aunis, the island is now attached to the department of Charente-Maritime and the Poitou-Charentes region and is divided into two cantons. It is low lying anf flat, beautiful in Summer but very exposed to Atlantic gales in the Winter.

The historic capital of the island is Saint-Martin-de-Re, which had with the neighbouring village a population of 5531 in 2008. It is the main port and has a sheltered harbour, seen here at the lower right of the picture.

Since May 19, 1988 the island has been connected to the mainland by an impressive road bridge. Until then the only access was by boat with St Martin the main port. Very much a tourist destination, the island is nicknamed "Re the white" because of the characteristic hue of its traditional houses. Other than tourism the island had a fishing fleet as well as oyster fisheries, but the biggest industry was salt production by evaporating sea water in large plat salt pans. It was transporting the salt that was one of the main factors in promoting the railway.

Saint-Martin-de-Ré has extensive fortifications, reflecting the strategic importance of the Île de Ré. During the Wars of Religion in the 1620s, Cardinal Richelieu ordered that the island be fortified as a counterweight to the Protestant nearby city of La Rochelle on the French mainland. This included a citadel at Saint Martin. After La Rochelle had been subdued, Saint-Martin's fortifications were largely demolished to remove its potential threat to royal power.

In 1627, an English invasion force under the command of George Villiers, Duke of Buckingham attacked the island in order to relieve the Siege of La Rochelle. After three months of combats in the Siege of Saint-Martin-de-Ré against the French under Marshal Toiras, the Duke was forced to withdraw in defeat.

Later, in the 1670s, the French engineer Vauban was commissioned to review and overhaul the island's defences and, as a result, Saint Martin was enclosed by extensive and modern walls and embankments.

This was done in three major phases ending in 1702 and the end result was an enclosed town capable of housing the island's population for a long siege.

Between 1873 and 1938, the prison in Saint-Martin de Re kept prisoners before they were shipped to the penal colonies in French Guiana or New Caledonia.

The island was heavily fortified as part of the Atlantic Wall during World War 2 to protect the important U Boat base at La Rochelle.

The main connection to the island was the ferry from La Rochelle to a rail served pier at Sablanceaux which was converted into a drive-on vehicle ferry when the railway closed. The terminal at Sablanceaux was at the far end of the island nearest to La Rochelle.

There were 40 000 journeys in 1947; this had risen to 872 000 in 1957 and 2,071,000 in 1967. It was getting to the stage where the ferries could no longer cope; a permanent road crossing was needed. A tunnel was considered, but in the end a road bridge was built, funded by the General Council of Charante Maritime. It is the second longest bridge in France, opening in 1988.

The postcard is a 1950's view of the ferry pier, in use from 1947 to 1988. La Rochelle is in the distance.

CHAPTER 3

THE RAILWAY

The Chemin de Fer Economiques de Charentes (CFEC) created a network of metre gauge railways in the departments of Charente and Charente-Maritime with the centre of the network in Saintes. The railways were declared a public utility on 30 January 1893. The lines on the Ile de Re were part of the system but of course were physically separate from it, with everything having to be transported to the island by boat which made the island lines very self-sufficient out of necessity.

41. ARS-EN-RÉ (Ile-de-Ré) — La Gare.

As early as 1877 the idea of giving the Ile de Re a railway was being mooted. The transfer of salt, fish and general goods and also of course passengers were the reasons put forward for building the railway; however it was not until 1898 that the line was officially inaugurated . It opened on July 9th 1898 after ten years of construction with a total length of 36.5km.

It linked all the communities on the island, but did not necessarily pass the centre of all the villages; the station serving Loix was located 4 km from the village. St Martin was at the end of a short branch line into the town where the trains reversed, and another short branch opened in 1899 terminated at the lighthouse, the 'Phare des Baleines'.

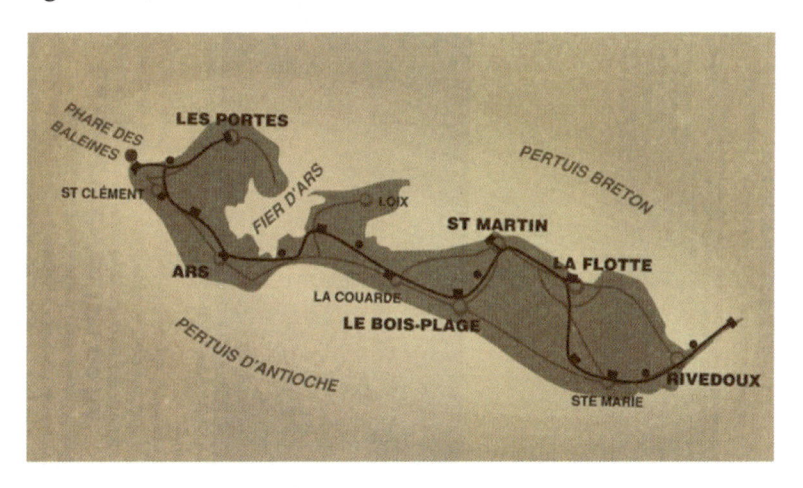

The closest point to the mainland was the pierhead at Sablanceaux where boats made the connection to La Rochelle, the line then running the length of the island to terminate at Les Portes. The loco sheds were at Ars de Re.

Passenger traffic was always the mainstay of the system, the island being very popular with tourists in the Summer months. The full journey from one end of the line to the other took on average two and a half to three hours so no speed records were being set, though the reversal at St Martin must have contributed to the slow rate of progress. The loco was always given a break at St Martin, cleaning the fire and oiling round the motion.

ILE de RÉ — Le Coligny à Quai St-Martin-de-Ré

It was for a time very successful and remained one of the symbols of the island, but in 1934 taxis and buses arrived on Re and the following year the little railway closed to passengers…it continued until 1937 for freight, almost entirely salt. During the Second World War the army of occupation and the the Todt organization revived the line to move materials for building defences, as well as the work force and soldiers …….passengers once more.

After the war, the shortage of fuel helped the railway continue to operate and then was it was transformed by the introduction of an Autorail but its new found prosperity was short lived and the rail network was closed in June 1947 and dismantled. A large part of it has been converted into cycle tracks.

Some remnants still exist: the station building at Ars, next to the port, and the locomotive shed there. A few traces also remain at the port of St. Martin and here and there by the side of the cycle tracks with the old rails transformed into fence posts.

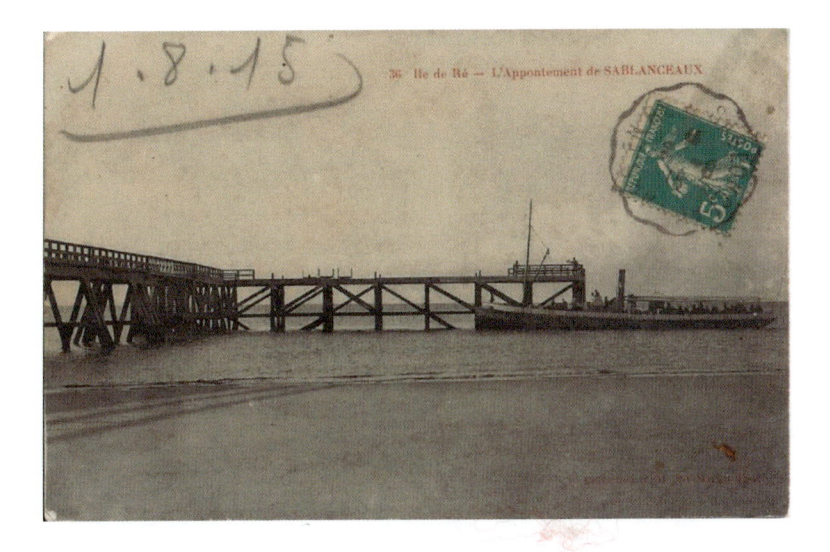

The pier at Sablanceaux, not an appealing prospect in the middle of winter!

CHAPTER 4

SABLANCEAUX PIER

This was where the Ile de Re railway terminated, on a narrow wooden pier along which the trains were propelled from Sanlanceaux station. Steamers picked up passengers for the transfer to the mainland, and also sailed on to serve St Martin de Re and St Marie. The boats in the postcards offered little protection to the passengers, so it was a good thing it was short crossing. The pier was constantly changing as the weather battered it, with some sections replaced in concrete in later years and a metal girder span being installed. It lasted until the demise of the railway in 1947, and was probably not greatly missed by those that had to use it.

At the end of the pier was Sablanceaux station; in the postcard the pier can be glimpsed on the left. It was a very exposed spot, so a reasonably substantial station building was provided.

10422. - Gare de SABLANCEAUX (Commune de Sainte-Marie. – Ile de Ré).
Un appontement permet d'assurer le passage avec La Pallice-Rochelle.

Although it is not clear from the photo's there must have been a run round loop at the station to enable the loco to propel the coaches along the pier.

The pier remained in use until the railway closed, increasingly unsatisfactory as an important transport connection and having a detrimental effect on the economy of the island. In 1947 it was replaced with a new ferry terminal and drive on – drive off ships which transformed the journey. We may get nostalgic about narrow gauge railways, but no one could argue that this was not an improvement!

The line of the old pier and railway can just be seen to the right of the new pier.

Finally in 1988 the island was connected to the main land with this magnificent bridge.

CHAPTER 5

ALONG THE LINE

The first settlement the line passed was Rivedoux, on the south coast of the island. This is a fairly sheltered place and lovely in Summer.

The trackbed is now a popular cycle path. The route passed the larger village of St Marie de Re but unfortunately I have been unable to find any pictures of the station here. The line then turned due north towards La Flotte.

La Flotte is on the north coast of the island, and from here the line ran west towards St Martin. The station was just a roadside halt with a small shelter. As always the café was close by!

The line ran past St Martin de Re, with a branch running into the two to which we will return. The main line turned south towards Le Bois-Plage on the south coast where there was another station.

177. - ILE de RÉ (Ch.-Inf.). - Le Bois-Plage - L'Express en Gare

The line then ran straight for several kilometres, past the halt at La Couarde until it was forced to turn sharply south where the island narrows beyond which was the small harbour town of Ars, which is where the locomotive sheds were located.

4259. Ile de Ré — Gare de LA COUARDE

41. ARS-EN-RÉ — La Gare

Remarkably, the station building at Ars survives.

Page 21

Beyond Ars the line followed the centre of the narrow island with another halt at St Clement and then a junction for a short 1.4km branch to the lighthouse 'Phare des Baleines' which stands on the extreme western end of the island. This branch was added in 1899, partly to service the lighthouse but also to open up that part of the coast, where stalls and pavilions were built for the visitors. Presumably the train backed down the branch before proceeding to Les Portes.

ILE DE RÉ. — Saint-Clément des Baleines. — Le Phare et les Chalets. — LL.

The buildings alongside the lighthouse were a telegraph station.

5 ILE DE RE. — Saint-Clément, le Sémaphore et le Phare des Baleines. — ND

The terminus of the railway was at Les Portes, pretty much at the end of the island. There was a small brick station building and a two track locomotive shed which still exists and is used by the local fire brigade.

Sadly this is another station that the postcard photographers seem to have ignored, so a modern picture will have to suffice.

CHAPTER 6

St MARTIN de RE

It was seeing postcards of St Martin that first attracted me to the railway as a prototype for a model. If you like boats and narrow gauge trains together, then look no further!

Believe it or not, that little building in the middle of the picture was the station.

As detailed earlier, St Martin was a fortified town enclosed by walls and ditches that can only really be appreciated from the air:

As this early map shows, it hasn't changed a great deal…

The railway branched off the main line just outside the town walls; unfortunately I don't have any details of the junction, but to allow running in both directions from St Martin a triangular junction would seem likeliest.

The branch then ran in a straight line towards the town and made use of an existing bridge across the defensive ditches, one of the most impressive entries into a town made by any narrow gauge railway…..

This is a train leaving the town.

St-Martin (Ile de Ré). - Porte Thouaras

42 St-MARTIN-de-RÉ - Entrée de la Ville, porte de Thoiras

ILE DE RE — Saint-Martin, la Porte Thoiras.

161 — Ile de RE. Saint-Martin. La Porte Thoiras. ND Phot

All the buildings predated the railway, they just laid the track along the existing road.

The railway is gone, but of course the bridge is still there.

From the bridge the railway ran in typical French fashion along the streets of the town towards the harbour.

When it arrived at the harbour, the line split to serve the quays on both sides. A tiny station was built pretty much in the middle of the road right by the quayside where the lines split, and it was here that the passenger trains reversed to continue their journey. Paddle steamers met the trains only a short walk away, it was a very convenient arrangement.

209. St-MARTIN (Ile de Ré) - Le bassin à flot et les quais

A single track can be seen running along the quayside. The station is just out of sight to the left.

ILE DE RÉ. — Saint-Martin-de-Ré — La Gare et le Bateau de La Rochelle. — LL.

This picture shows convicts disembarking from a ship. Happily it is also an excellent view of the station building.

25. - Ile de Ré. - St-MARTIN. - Entrée du Port

Page 35

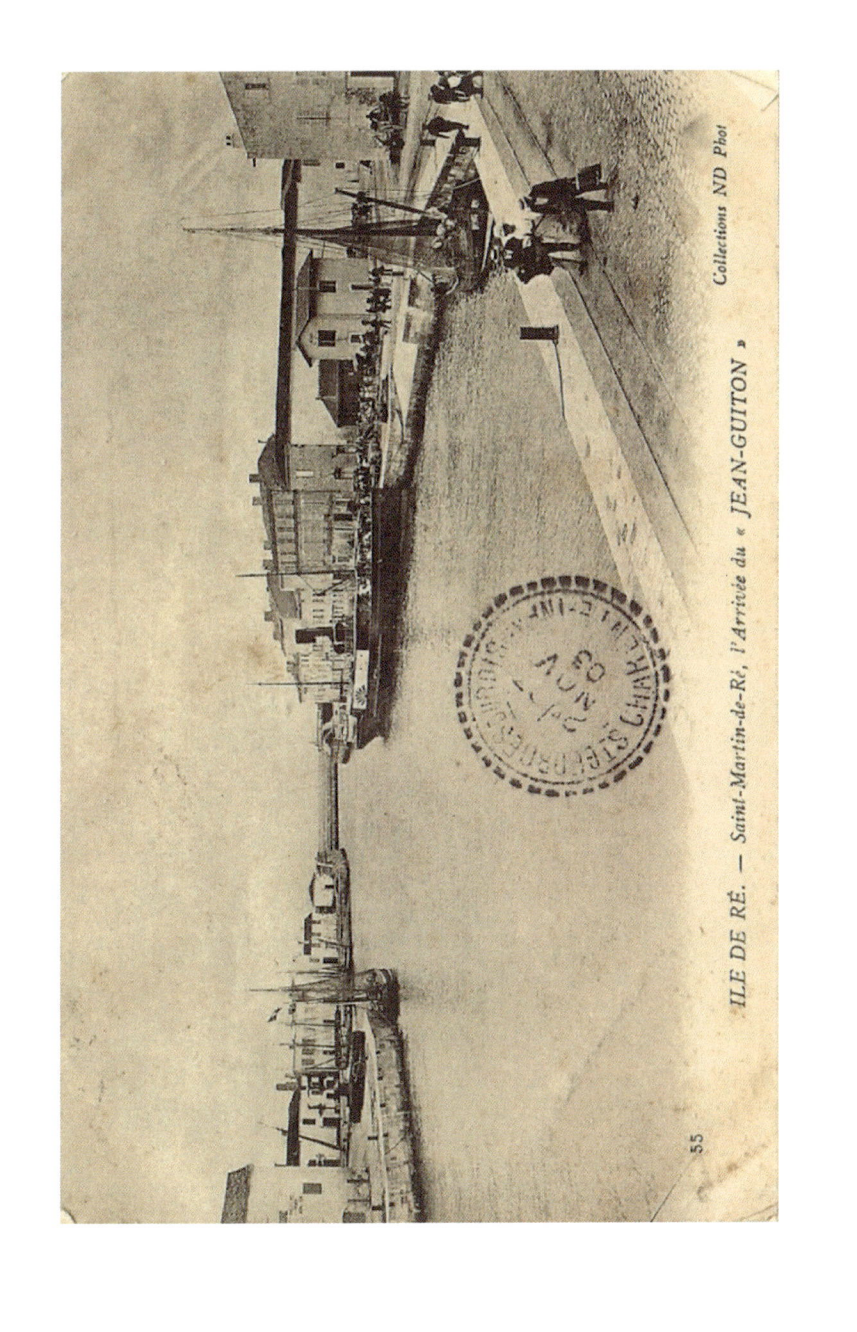

ILE DE RÉ. — Saint-Martin-de-Ré, l'Arrivée du « JEAN-GUITON »

Collections ND Phot

Other than the removal of the station building – understandably! – the scene is very little changed today although the boats are rather different. The station was behind the articulated lorry on the left. .

CHAPTER 6

LOCOMOTIVES & ROLLING STOCK.

The only steam locomotives to work on the island were Corpet Louvet 030 tanks which handled all the traffic; the whole of the Charentes narrow gauge system was operated using only these loco's, the ones on the island presumably being taken back to the mainland when major overhaul was required.

The short lived Autorail was a De Dion JM4 dating from 1932.

All the pictures show four wheeled coaches, and that trains often ran mixed.

The nearest preserved example of a Corpet Louvet tank of the type used on the Ile de Re is 'Cambrai' which is in the museum at Irthlingborough, Northants, in England. These pictures give an idea of what one of the island loco's would have looked like. She was built in 1888, slightly later than the island engines, but is a very similar type. She came to the U.K. to work on an ironstone line in Leicestershire.

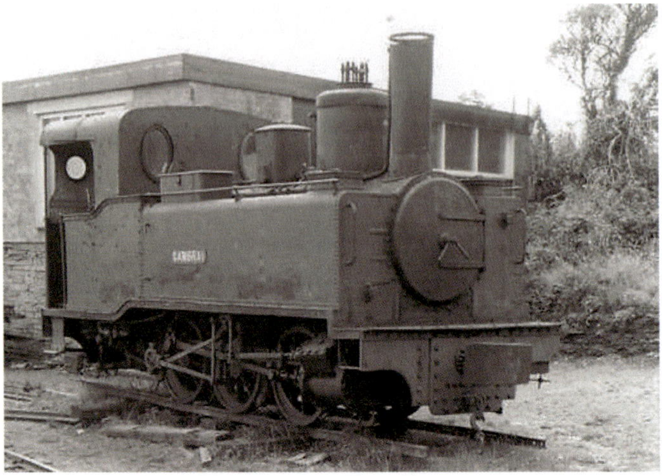
CAMBRAI

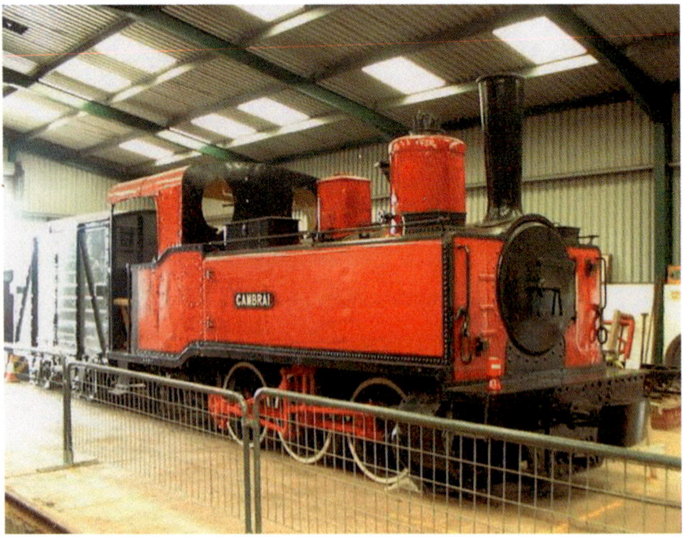
CAMBRAI

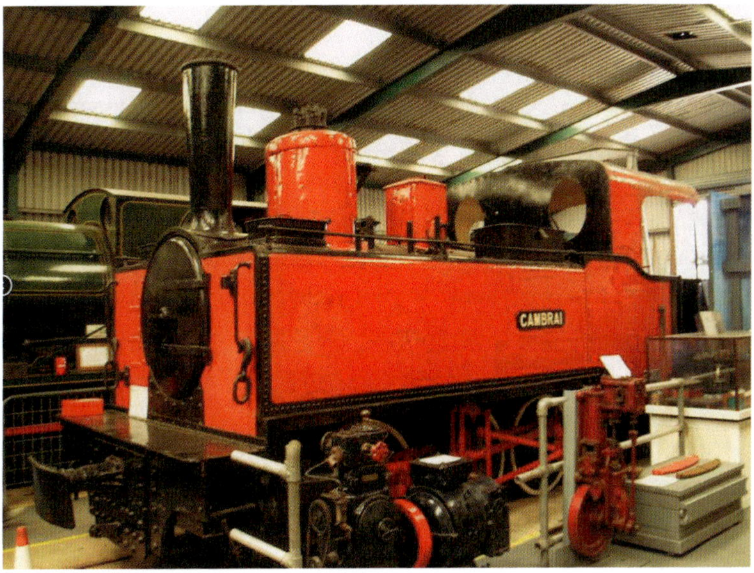
CAMBRAI

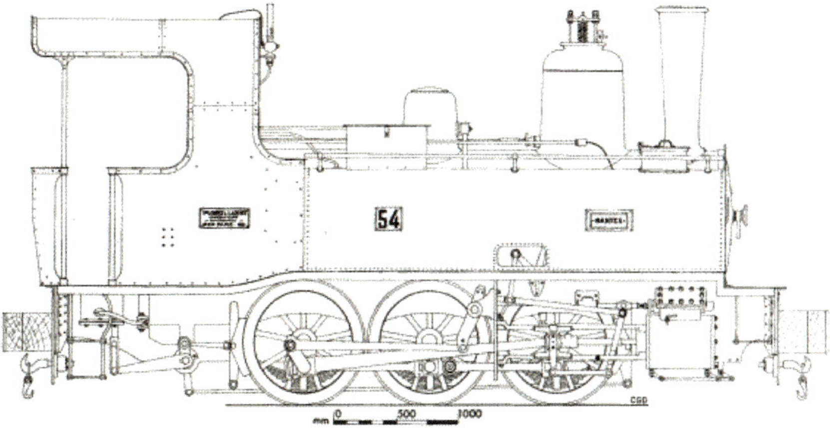
54
CGD
mm 0 500 1000

BOATS AND SHIPS

The 'Jean Guitton' of 1867 and the 'Coligny' of 1876 were the two paddle steamers that connected the island to the mainland when the railway opened, sailing to La Rochelle from St Martin de Re. The former was scrapped in the nineteenth century but the 'Coligny' sailed on until 1937 after being refitted in 1920; she is certainly the steamer seen in many of the postcards. The steamers carried first and second class passengers and freight but of course the service was dependant on the tides. Diesel powered vessels were introduced in 1949, and continued until the road bridge was opened in 1988. There was also the ferry from the pier at Sablanceaux which crossed to La Rochelle and was replaced by a drive-on car ferry when the tramway closed in 1947. This ceased to operate in 1988 on the opening of the new bridge.

Two views of the 1867 paddle steamer 'Jean Guitton'.

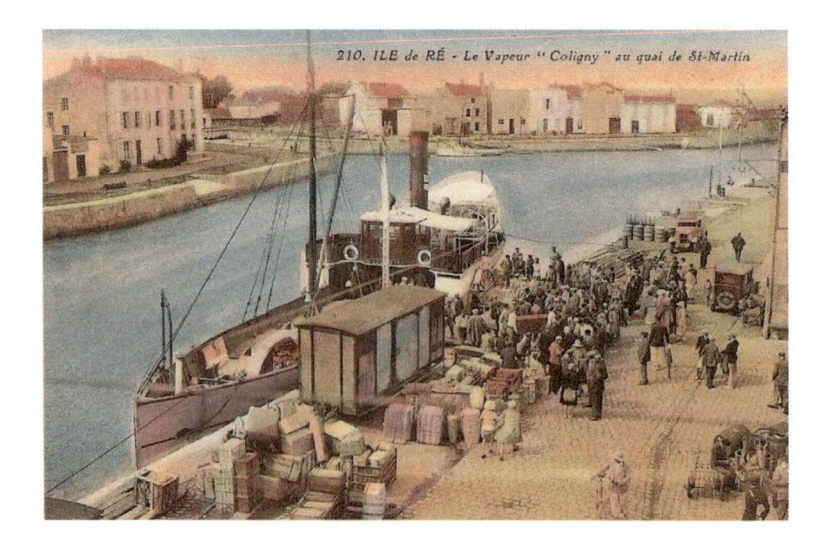

The dangers of trusting coloured postcards! The lower one looks a lot more accurate to me.

Page 43

The 'Coligny' at St Martin – what a fabulous funnel!

12075. Ile de Ré. SAINT-MARTIN-DE-RÉ — Le "Coligny" à Quai

ILE D'OLERON

CHAPTER 1
INTRODUCTION

The island of Oleron is located in the Atlantic Ocean off the coast of Charente-Maritime where it is part of the Charente archipelago.

The second largest greater metropolitan French island after Corsica, 30 km long by 8 km wide, it has an area of 1 174 km 2 and more than 21 000 inhabitants.

Administratively, the island of Oleron now belongs to the department of Charente-Maritime and is divided into two cantons. Its current capital is Saint-Pierre d'Oléron, the main commercial centre of the island. Under the old regime it was the city of Château d'Oléron, head of the local government and housing the garrison of the island which fulfilled this function.

Since 19 March 1966, the island has been connected to the mainland by a road bridge; at 3021 m long (the third longest bridge in France after that of the Ile de Re and that of Saint-Nazaire) it is the oldest bridge in France linking an island to the mainland.

Celebrated by Pierre Loti, Oléron is called "light" because of its high level of sunshine throughout the year.

Eleanor of Aquitaine stayed at the Château d'Oléron castle in 1199 . She remained there for some time, writing a series of maritime rules knows as the 'Roles of Oleron' before retiring to the Abbey of Fontevraud , where she died in 1204 .

In February 1625 , the Protestant Soubise captured the island after occupying the island of Ré . A few months later, the Duke of Guise organized a landing back to the island, supported by the Dutch and English fleets.

The island was one of the last pockets of German resistance during World War II and was finally released late in April 1945 1 during a landing of nearly 8000 men . Almost all were recruits from the Resistance, the regular army being absorbed by the fighting in the Vosges. Promoted to lieutenant colonel in March 1945, René Babonneau took command of 158 e RI, at whose head he took part in this operation.

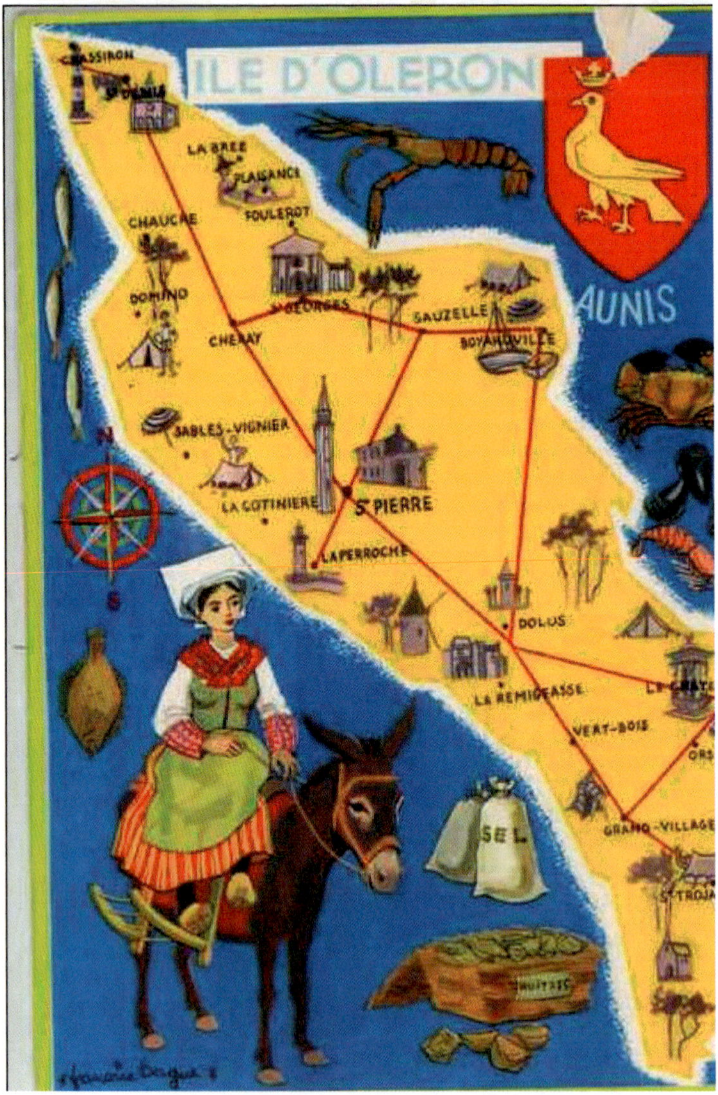
ILE D'OLERON
CHASSIRON
S^T DENIS
LA BREE
PLAISANCE
FOULEROT
CHAUCRE
DOMINO
S^T GEORGES
CHERAY
SAUZELLE
BOYARDVILLE
AUNIS
SABLES-VIGNIER
LA COTINIERE
S^T PIERRE
LAPERROCHE
DOLUS
LA REMIGEASSE
VERT-BOIS
GRAND-VILLAGE
SEL
HUITRES

CHAPTER 2

BACKGROUND TO BUILDING THE RAILWAY

In the early 19th century, the metalled roads are non-existent on the island of Oleron. In 1841, the inauguration of the national road which connects the Castle to Chassiron improved the situation.

This same year 1841 saw the birth of "the Islander", first transport company created by Jacques Bouineau. Each day a connection by sailboat was made between the Castle and The Chapus. Each week three other connections were provided between La Rochelle and Saint-Denis , Boyardville and the castle.

In 1882, Andre Bouineau founded the "Company Oleronnaise of Navigation" with five steamships sailing between the Castle and the mainland. However, to the interior of the island there was only one coach which had difficulty on the muddy roads of the island.

In 1875, a first draft of an underwater tunnel connecting the mainland to the island was made, to be operated using a steam tram. The projected tunnel, which would have connected the Chapus to Ors, was abandoned because the gradients would have been too steep. A second similar project, proposed by the administration in 1877, was also abandoned ; the use of a metal bridge with a lifting central span had also been studied, but not proceeded with.

In 1900, under pressure from Andre Bouineau, it was decided to construct a railway connecting Saint-Trojan and Saint-Denis with a branch to Boyardville. A concession of 60 years was then granted to the Bouineau company.

At the inauguration, the line had a length of 46.5 kilometres and had 28 stops.

CHAPTER 3

THE RAILWAY

The railway was part of the Charentes Economiques system in the same way as the Ile se Re lines.

Five locomotives were used for the entire network, Corpet-Louvet 030's weighing 14.5 tonnes. At the outset, 16 coaches were used: 4 composites (first and second class), 8 second class, and 4 with a postal section. This allowed the formation of four complete trains, when there were no repairs in progress. For the transport of goods, 34 wagons were used: 8 vans, 4 open wagons, 12 low side opens, 8 flat cars wagons and 2 timber wagons with a cross beam.

TRAIN SERVICE

Four round trips daily were made between Saint-Trojan and Saint-Denis, and three return trips between Boyardville and Saint-Pierre. Each day nearly 400 kilometres were travelled. Four trains were needed with one locomotive in reserve or under repair. The average speed was 20 km/h taking into account the number of stops ; between Sauzelle and Boyardville the speed was only 14 Km/h because of the length of the train and the very tight curves on this section.

When the war broke out in 1914 most of the employees are mobilized and some of the locomotives are sent to the front. After the war, to meet deficits the service was very much reduced: now there were only two return trips on the main line and two between Saint-Pierre and Boyardville.

The staff dealing with the railway were divided into three categories. There were thirteen working on or responsible for the trains: firemen, drivers and a few others doing shunting, dispatching an so on. There were nine men involved in the maintenance of the track and infrastructure. There were finally twenty four staff working at the stations and in the repair and maintenance workshops.

By 1927 there was no more than one single return trip, the buses now competing with the train. The bus took just as long to do the same journey but it was cheaper and things got worse for the railway when in 1929 the buses were brought under local authority control. By 1935 the passenger service on the railway had ceased, and as freight had also declined alarmingly the railway was abandoned.

288. ILE D'OLÉRON (Ch.-Inf.) — Saint-Trojan-les-Bains, la Gare du Tram et le Port

Page 54

CHAPTER 4

ALONG THE LINE

Saint-Trojan was the beginning of the line; the station was located at the entrance of the town near the Port. The little terminus has a tiny station building with an attached goods shed, and a single road loco shed with a metal water tank on wooden supports adjacent to it. There was a tiny toilet building next to the station building.

The single track split into three loops, the furthest from the building having a wagon weighbridge. The three loops joined again into a single track at the end of the line.

This pretty little station looks just like a model railway in the postcards which were nearly all taken from the cliff top looking down on the station.

Ils d'Oléron. — 171. SAINT-TROJAN-LES-BAINS
La gare
ÉDIT. SERVOIS.

Ile d'Oléron. - St-TROJAN. - La Gare et le Port

53. Ile d'Oléron. — St-Trojan-les-Bains. — La Gare

Although it looks attractive it must have been a bleak spot in the winter.

ILE D'OLÉRON — SAINT-TROJAN — Le Port et la Gare

Page 58

Saint-Trojan station was well photographed, but sadly the same cannot be said of the rest of the line.

Leaving Saint-Trojan the railway ran towards Chateau Oleron passing request stops at Petit Village and Grand Village, surrounded by salt marshes.

The channel of the Ors was crossed by a concrete bridge, and after the request stop at Bordeliniere the line arrived at the two stations serving Le Chateau D'Oleron.

On the outskirts of the first station the track divided into two branches which formed a triangle with three parallel tracks as the third side. This allowed many shunting movements, including the complete reversal of a train. A track ran onto the wharf to facilitate the transfer of goods between the train and the boats of the Oleronnaise company. Le Chateau D'Oleron had two distinct stations: Chateau-wharf and Chateau-Port.

2236. Charente-Infre — Le Château — Le Port

On the way out of Le Chateau D'Oleron, the first stop was optional, located only 368 meters from the station of Chateau-Port, then there was a second request stop before reaching the halt at Gaconniere, which became a full station in 1913.

In Saint-Pierre the first stop was the halt of Saint-Pierre - La Cotiniere which served the neighbourhood of Bel Air, Maisonneuve and La Cotiniere. Two branch lines served the wine merchant Gresseau-Peponnet and the distillery Soudois. The line then continued to the station in Saint-Pierre, one of the most important on the line.

Freight here was mainly made up of gross tonnage and the goods platform was enlarged in 1916. The station building had a cafe, and was here that the railway workshops were located.

From Saint-Pierre in the direction of Saint-Denis the next station was that of Sauzelle, which in fact was nowhere near the village of Sauzelle. The line separated into two there, so first we'll follow that which ran north.

Saint-Georges station was located very close to the town, and then came the village of Le Bree where the station was located away from the village, in a place called "Le Breuil".

The station of Saint-Denis was the terminus of the line, but it continued in the direction of the harbour. The silting of the harbour affected goods traffic on this section of the line until it dwindled to almost nothing.

Now back to the line which connects Sauzelle to Boyardville. There were halts at Four Paths and Saurine before arriving at the terminus of Boyardville. This station was busy as the trains connected with steamships transporting passengers from La Rochelle, as well as coal and fertilizers for import and fish, Cognac, Pineau, wine and salt for export.

26 — BOYARDVILLE (Ile d'Oléron) - Vue du Port

CHAPTER 5

SAINT TROJAN MINATURE RAILWAY

The miniature railway at Saint-Trojan , which links this town to the tip of the 'Point de Gatseau' has nothing to do with the metre gauge railway. It was constructed in 1963, primarily from military equipment transferred by the area after the dismantling of the Maginot line. It carries a little under 70,000 passengers per year, between Easter and the end of September.

Printed in Great Britain
by Amazon.co.uk, Ltd.,
Marston Gate.